WRITINGS OF AN
Eccentric Gypsy

WRITINGS OF AN
Eccentric Gypsy

By Sandra Lesser

SUNSTONE PRESS

SANTA FE

© 2011 by Sandra Lesser. All Rights Reserved.

No part of this book may be reproduced in any form or by any electronic or mechanical means including information storage and retrieval systems without permission in writing from the publisher, except by a reviewer who may quote brief passages in a review.

Sunstone books may be purchased for educational, business, or sales promotional use. For information please write: Special Markets Department, Sunstone Press, P.O. Box 2321, Santa Fe, New Mexico 87504-2321.

Printed on acid free paper

Library of Congress Cataloging-in-Publication Data

Lesser, Sandra, 1947-
 Writings of an eccentric Gypsy / by Sandra Lesser.
      p. cm.
 ISBN 978-0-86534-799-1 (softcover : alk. paper)
 I. Title.
PS3612.E8187W75 2011
811'.6--dc22

WWW.SUNSTONEPRESS.COM
SUNSTONE PRESS / POST OFFICE BOX 2321 / SANTA FE, NM 87504-2321 /USA
(505) 988-4418 / ORDERS ONLY (800) 243-5644 / FAX (505) 988-1025

CONTENTS

PREFACE / vii

BECOMING A BUTTERFLY / ix
GARDEN OF LIFE / x
PHASES / xii
LIFE CHANGES / xiv
THE TREE AND ME / xvii
THE WAY / xxvi
TROUBLE FRIEND / xxvii
THE LONGER WE LOOK / xxix
TAROT / xxxiii
BEAR'S PRAYER / xxxv
INVITATION TO DEATH / xxxvii
THOSE YEARS / xxxix
THE TOAD AND THE WATER LILY / xl
WHO'S THERE / xliii
BEFORE OUR FUTURE / xlv
PRESIDENTIAL WOE / xlvi
THE ATTIC / xlix
CREATIVE CRITICISM / li
VIRGINITY / liii
MESSAGE FOR DYLAN / liv
OLD DAYS / lvi
MY PLACE / lviii
FULFILLMENT / lxi

GYPSY NOTES / lxiii

PREFACE

I have decided to catalogue and preserve the many poems I have written over the years. Whether they come "from me" or "through me" they absolutely reflect the emotions I felt at the time and the unusual adventures I was either forced to or decided I wanted to embark upon. The decisions were mine and I traveled a road which led me to the place where I am today.

There are many forms of reflecting on and healing from life's experiences—mine happens to be my own form of expression through words—true poetry or simple rhyme—it's almost like writing a diary—you can look back on it, see in writing what you have been through and read for yourself how you have handled each situation and grown through it all.

As I have finished my own book of writings, "diary", my hope is that I can share it with anyone who might benefit from it or be inspired to take the time to find and express in your own way how unique and special you really are. I think of my collection as "Eccentric Gypsy Poems" because that is how I see myself. You can name yourself and take it from there. Remember, everyone has a different story to tell, and if they are willing to share that story with you, you just might learn something and be able to pass it on at the right "Gypsy" moment. Thank you for getting this far and my worldly, somewhat eccentric, poems will follow.

BECOMING A BUTTERFLY

Furry and aimless, it absently wanders
through daylight and darkness alone
Surviving the occasional rains and drought
and detouring paths of stone

Seeking a solitude earned by its peers
yet to itself painfully unknown
Hiding inside of itself for no other reason
than to be fearful of a world overgrown

Challenging time in its self-made envelope
a subtle change takes place
Though unaware, it is becoming apparent
there is an underlying, beautiful face

Slowly fading, giving way
like the transition from denim to lace
It prepares itself with a new-found strength
to unfold with dignity and grace

Awakening to sunshine, sensing life at its touch
it is understandably shy
When at one time it was familiar only with the ground
it now feels closer to the sky

Be free, someone calls, and don't look back
you can go anywhere if you'll only try
So with little fear, it forgot how to crawl
and instinctively learned how to fly

GARDEN OF LIFE

She planted a garden a long time ago
Expecting the most glorious things to grow
No matter it wasn't the right time of year
Everyone knows the young have no fear

She knew the perennials were not threatened by rain
But if they failed this time, they would come back again
So she sat back and watched, let nature take its course
Waiting for the beauty to break through with great force

Strange things happened as the seasons changed
The garden was not as she had arranged
Where there should have been roses, there appeared a weed
With no indication of where it might lead

There was not always time for special attention—
After all, isn't nature God's invention?
Yet her instincts told her something was wrong
All living things should be healthy and strong

As Springtime approached and determination took over
She cleared out the crabgrass and made way for the clover
Then, as if by magic, Summer arrived
And the whole garden bloomed–it's just beginning to thrive

So when Winter comes it will pose no threat
What she has learned she will never forget
While its growth may at times have seemed belated
It's by far the most beautiful thing she has created

She should be proud
She has so much to show
From that garden she planted
A long time ago

PHASES

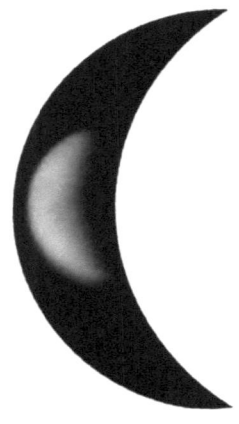
You saw the Moon at quarter full
and wondered why it bothered to rise
In the haze of the fog and the shadow of the clouds
it seemed to be telling you lies

Yet it held your attention and promised to grow brighter
as it challenged you to wait
but while you weren't looking it disappeared from view
you were only a moment too late

So you forgot that lonely disk in the sky
and went fearlessly on your way
and soon you saw it had doubled its size
and thought maybe it's here to stay

Determined to make sense of its timely message
you watched it change before your eyes
but before you had time to believe in its powers
there was a three-quarter Moon in the skies

Its changes, you thought, seemed similar to your own
yet you still didn't quite make the connection
It was like looking through the clearest of glass
and suddenly seeing your own reflection

It was beckoning you to wait once more
as it again took second place to the Sun
and true to its word, you saw it smile down at the World
as if to say "I've just begun"!

For through all of its changes, it always finds peace
a full Moon has nothing to lose
The Stars are its friends, it is truly ageless
and there will always be someone else to amuse

Life Changes

I know I'm not the best companion right now
but I have been a good wife and friend
There are some disturbances in our life
but enough for our relationship to end?

I cherish all the things you have given me
whether fancy wrapped or in a paper sack
While I could never have been quite as generous
I like to think I've given you something back

Now I'm a victim of an assault on my body
I can't share with you how it affects my mind
Sometimes I'm just angry because I'm a woman
and I'm not ready for changes of this kind

I struggle to contain my confusing temper
I try not to create a life of disharmony
I don't sleep and everything I would like to do
becomes much harder—almost impossible to me

Too bad there isn't an instruction manual
for women who one day become my age
Should they be tossed out like some child's toy
or be protected like a lioness in a cage

I can't explain how the world looks different
or why I see things from a different view
but at times I sense you might understand
something similar could be happening to you

All I know is I'm really fighting hard
to keep believing what is in my heart
There isn't anything is this world that's worth
tearing each other's lives apart

Neither of us has the perfect answer
I guess we could do as others have done
but without trying to compromise with each other
have we lost…or have we won?

I don't want to control your final choices
and I can't control what's happening to me
If it's more than you can deal with
I can understand your need to be free

If that's how it is, I will accept
but I won't apologize for how it ends
Someday, somewhere down the road
I hope we can again be friends

THE TREE AND ME

At the very top of a lonely mountain
there stand a Tree, majestic and tall
The only thing near it for miles and miles
is a Flower, fragile and small

The Flower, not the prettiest by far,
likes to think it is there for a reason
It becomes more content as it weathers each storm
through every passing season

The Tree is first to see the sun rise
it has always been that way
The Flower, awakening from the dark of its shadow
only then sees the light of day

The Tree never worries much about storms
or the threat of erosion and such
for it has withstood the test of time
and managed to remain untouched

The Flower, though it would like to believe
its position is equally secure,
looks up the hillside at the powerful Tree
and cannot be so sure

The Tree, by its very existence,
provides shelter for its friends
but its limbs at times feel the weight of its vigil
through a multitude of sins

Neither cares less about visiting strangers
they want only for time to stand still
yet the Flower greets them, unaware of the dangers,
on their way to the top of the hill

The inevitable freezing nights will come
and they'll invent a silent game-
which of us will survive up here
and which of us is to blame

Everyone knows a Flower will wilt
when it can no longer draw a breath
or when one of the visiting strangers
one day tramples it to death

The Tree stands helpless on its mountain top
as it watches the Flower dying
and as the raindrops fall from its hearty leaves
you could swear the tree was crying

Still, you will find at the top of the mountain
an older and wiser Tree
with its roots slowly growing closer
to the place where the Flower used to be

The mighty Tree still stands atop
its strategic mountain site
It has known the sun through many days
watched the moon protect the night

Rain has fallen hard upon its leaves
at times it was icy cold
but still you will see its branches swaying
as if they were meant to scold

Many visitors have come and gone
some leaving behind their mark
The paper makers keep their distance though
the Tree can see them in the dark

Change is apparent—its roots seem to groan
the air is different somehow
Those who claim to be the guardians
have no idea what is happening now

The Tree's best friend, the little Flower,
still comes alive in the spring
It shakes off the sleep, lifts its weary head
and defiantly begins to sing

Never having been as strong as its mentor
always surprised and happy to see
the shadow it has come to know so well
the one that is cast by the Tree

In actual age it is Fifty and proud
it shouts now—let the changes come
for the Flower has finally grown tall enough
and the Tree has bent over some

They believe they're lucky to be alive
they're grateful for the things that be
and this Spring the Flower celebrates life
with a toast to the mighty Tree

This year the Flower approaches an age
it never thought could be
It has survived the unpredictable storms
in the shelter of the Tree

The Tree hates things left unfinished
the Flower believes things never are
the Tree planted solid in the soil
the Flower careless as a shooting star

The visitors are much gentler now
almost treading on sacred ground
covering each footstep as they follow the path
listening to every sound

Still they will stumble as the Tree expects
the Flower feeling their pain
but the sweetness of its nectar
overpowers the acrid scent of the rain

The colors of the Flower are vibrant
when threatening clouds drift away
Its ancestors quietly haunt and demand
ignorance of the old shades of gray

The Tree observes the changes in terrain
with a skeptical, uneasy eye
It is sure it has reached its tallest height
the whole picture now is the sky

The Flower wants to shout to the Tree
"Your vigilance should not be tested-
a Sentinel's patience is its only reward"
the Tree feels the Earth is infested

With blustery winds and quaking land
the Flower still shivers in the night
The spirit of the Tree in its armor-like bark
is prepared to stand and fight

All each can say is perhaps there's still time
to see what is meant to be
as Springtime once again embraces
the Flower and the mighty Tree

In the chilling frost of the millennium winter
the Flower and the Tree parted ways
Inside their hearts, they knew it would happen
through their idleness, they were counting the days

One on one they were apparently surviving
side by side they were warding off threats
The Tree wanted to explore the Land
the Flower wanted to understand their regrets

A Weed in disguise invaded the place
the Tree and the Flower always shared
The Tree's branches reached out as expected
and the Flower no longer cared

On the hilltop, their sacred place,
nothing could stop the erosion
As with all living things disease sets in
and confusion follows the explosion

The Winds, the Sun, the Rain and the Snow
no longer affect the Flower and the Tree
The saga may have ended, they may grow on their own
or die, whatever is meant to be

The mighty Tree still fights to this day
its survival is all that has mattered
The Flower, while wilting, still looks up to the Tree
even though their hilltop has been shattered

At the very top of a lonely mountain
the Tree still looks down on its land
It has for so many years now
held its heart in its branch–like hand

From its highest lookout it has bitterly observed
yet it has not itself been able to roam
Knowledge and boredom now challenge its strength
its roots wanting desperately to leave home

Before it can travel it must consider its friend
the Flower it has always protected
along with the love the Flower embraces
which the Tree has off-handedly rejected

It's not about the disease that has set in
or the worry about what certainly will come
It's a weariness that plagues the stoic Tree
and the Flower is sad but not dumb

The elements threaten, the struggle is too hard
the Tree's roots aren't so deep after all
It has almost become a one-sided fight
all the Tree can do now is stall

Without the Flower and the mighty Tree
the mountain top will echo and stand bare
Their separation might be their destruction
but of course, who on Earth will care?

By some miracle or sheer determination
the Flower is still blooming each year
It looks up at the mountain from time to time
to see if the mighty Tree could be near

The hillside has changed for the Tree has paled
yet the ghostly birds sing an occasional song
They send to both a magical message
that neither the Tree nor the Flower was wrong

Without all the years of growth
that the Tree and the Flower endured
They would not understand the ground that held them
was never meant to be disturbed

The Flower looks at its threatened future
it hopes to leave seeds behind
The Tree is struggling for the world to remember
it was tough but wanted to be kind

If how they first began their journey
and their legacy is meant to last
They will always respect each other
looking to the future—never to the past.

THE WAY

The circuses, they close their tents short of sundown
The lions and tigers, they have eaten the clown
The jugglers and the tumblers want a showdown
And they tell you to get out of the way

The trains, they once had determination
Now they've forgotten the reason for their destination
They're hoping the next stop will be their last station
They can't make it another day

The stones in the graveyard, they once led me home
Now they weep in the shadows of weeds overgrown
Looking for them makes me know I'm alone
They can no longer show me the way

Only the dealmakers know what's real
There's even more now for them to steal
The losers, they don't know how to feel
And, of course, they don't know what to say

The clocks, they still tick away the time
But the numbers on their faces, they're out of line
Can't wait around—don't know if they'll chime
Sorry—I'm on my way

TROUBLED FRIEND

An unexpected turn for the worse
or the inevitable, who knows
Though I knew it was coming I thought she could cope
but it seems she can't and it shows

She could push the button marked self-destruct
and leave him to be free
but how would she know if she were not around
that she had relieved him of his misery

Yet to stand by and watch only makes things worse
and when she suffers, I suffer more
Why is it she cares more about him than herself
and then wonders what it's all for

They say late is better that never
and in my heart I certainly concur
He was all that she wanted, what happened to them
better yet, what happened to her

I won't say he never gave it a chance
and I can't say he didn't try
She just couldn't handle her part of the bargain
and she will never understand why

With all due respect for her recently lost love
and all that it represents
She savors her dignity, plays second to no one
and strikes out only in self defense

I've advised her to put it all in the past
and move on to something else
But she politely reminds me this is one of those times
she must find things out for herself

Yet as I look back and reflect on a time
when my life was not trouble free
I remember how comforting it was just to know
that I had a friend like me

THE LONGER WE LOOK

As we follow this fast moving world
we will never all agree
Some things appear to be an illusion, but
the longer we look, the more we see

Watching clouds changing shapes
looking closely at the bark of a tree
Wild animals in their own private domain
the longer we look, the more we see

Everything changing or standing still
reflecting on what's fake and what's reality
All that seems complicated is really simple
the longer we look, the more we see

The shape of a rock
the movement of the sea
A flock of birds taking flight
the longer we look, the more we see

An apparently solid piece of glass
a face held in captivity
Nothing replaces our imagination
the longer we look, the more we see

Everything has a life of its own
a kind of beauty meant to be free
All can bring pleasure as we've never known
the longer we look, the more we see

Looking through rose colored glasses
only disguises what we perceive
All we desire is right there in our eyes
the longer we look, the more we see

TAROT

The King of Pentacles, how serious is he
in his search for contentment and love?
The Page of Cups is his latest companion
but he wonders—Who is She?

She's a fair-haired lady longing for peace
always wondering which way to turn.
She's looking for answers and years of reasons
and hoping—expecting to learn

She turns to her music and the cards
casts her destiny to fate.
She also turns away from the things
she knows she will eventually hate.

But as the cards reveal themselves
and the songs continue to be
The very essence of herself makes her wonder
Who is She?

The King tries to answer and make the cards fall
without influence and what he could call
his affection and all that could be said.
Yet the Page remains stable and dubious in her thoughts
as she ponders where the past years might have led.

Her Social surroundings confuse her
so many silently watching and few encouraging her to be free
While so much depends on her frame of mind
and years of misdirected ability.

Her own cards tell her she must be what she can be
keep her sanity to the very end
Stay with the one who can understand why
she eternally questions and asks her friends
Who is She?

With time growing shorter and the storm within her restless
she begins to see things differently.
The King remains patient, observing the changes
for he knows in time she will answer the question
Who is She?

Perhaps one day the cards will fall in a manner she can accept
and she will dance to the music of those who are free
or will they once again play a trick and win
and she will find she is not what she appears to be.

BEAR'S PRAYER

If I were the keeper of animals
each would be peaceful like the dove
If I were the keeper of memories
the world would be full of love

If I were the keeper of anger
If I were the keeper of doubt
If I were the keeper of children
no one would be without

If I were the keeper of Spirit
If souls were under my care
If I were the keeper of necessities
there would always be enough to share

If I were the keeper of animals
If I could make dreams come true
I'd wish all my friends could be
as happy as I have been with you

INVITATION TO DEATH

Come to my party on the seventh of June
and celebrate the rising of the Moon.

Bring a partner or come alone
either way, you'll be on your own.

I'll send a black limo so you can arrive in style
don't plan to leave early, you'll be here for a while.

Walk softly in this place you've never been before
there are no walls, no ceilings, no floors.

Pieces of broken mirrors will reflect
and this is not a place you will find respect

There will be unseen faces and familiar voices
yet the silence will not be disturbed by noises.

Costumes and disguises will serve no purpose
you'll be recognized from within—not by the surface.

The fragrance of roses will numb your senses
and you might think you were invited under false pretenses.

Curiousity will surely keep you amused
any reasonable request will not be refused.

So clear your head of memories, keep an open mind
this is your chance to completely unwind.

From empty glasses we will drink to a toast
and soon after midnight you will meet your host.

You've been invited before, but you sent your regrets
something about repaying your debts.

You'll attend this time, I'm willing to bet
and it will be a party you will never forget.

I did not start writing my form of poetry until I was in my late 20's and never knew that my mother enjoyed doing the same. After my father died, I realized that my mother still had feelings for a man I had known since childhood and cared for very much. They were both married then so their love was unfulfilled. Knowing my father would not disapprove, after his death, I got them together, just as friends (I think) and they talked about those days once again before she died. I later wrote the poem entitled "Those Years" which I proudly dedicate to her. Even later, I found her old high school history book dated 1923 which was full of her poetry (she obviously did not study history—almost every page was covered with her writings!) I have included one in her memory. I wish every day now that we had shared our special talent while she was alive. This is my way of thanking her for the gift and the courage to hopefully give it all meaning to you and your love ones.

THOSE YEARS

I met you when you were not free
I left you with more than one memory
I bet you never had time to think of me
those many years

I looked for you among the crowd
and at times I wished I could cry out loud
for what we were feeling was not allowed
for so many years

We made a promise we would hurt no one
though inside we hurt for a love undone
We kept our promise and as life passed us by
we came to wonder why

I raised my family and you raised yours
then life lost its meaning—became a chore
You were so close yet so far from my door
those many years

And then late in life I found myself free
wondering what had happened to me
There was no time left for sympathy
after so many years

Times had changed, I could now tell the world
of a love I had hidden since I was just a girl
but though you still loved me, you were not free
after all those years

We still have our dreams and our children too
they don't have to know what we've been through
It must be enough that I have thought of you
those many years

I still look for you among the crowd
and when I'm lonely, I do cry out loud
for that feeling that was not allowed
all those years

They brought me many tears…those years

Darling it's a dark and dreary night
And in the sky there are no stars.
But still I love you with all my might
No matter where you are.

I'd be the happiest girl in the world
If this one thing I knew
That while I'm thinking of you tonight
You might be thinking of me too.

It seems like ages since I've seen you
Though just a while it's been my dear.
But darling I'm telling you at times
It seems like at most a year.

I wish the time would sometime come
Though it never will be it seems
When we could have that little home
Which is the heart of all my dreams.

Goodnight sweetheart
Though you cannot hear what I say
If the Heavenly Father is willing
Perhaps you will hear me someday.

—Dorothy Louise Berrie

THE TOAD AND THE WATER LILY

For every water lily, there is born a toad
Hopping around is not easy when he's carrying a load.

When the toad becomes heavy, he stops to take a rest
And the lily he lands on looks uncomfortable at best.

He looks around, fears it's too far to jump
If he misses his target, he could easily land on his rump.

So he decides to settle in and croak for a while
Asking permission is just not his style.

Now the lily is gracious as she's always been
But as time passes on, her patience grows thin.

The toad's weight becomes heavier and it's no wonder
He has come to take advantage of the "land down under".

Why is it a surprise that when he's decided to stay
She politely invites him to be on his way.

Come on, let's admit that as far as toads go
Once in a while there's one we're reluctant to let go.

Perhaps we should be flattered
pay it further mind
Then again, gracious water lilies
aren't so easy to find.

WHO'S THERE?

A false feeling of serenity surrounds this usually watchful eye
it's like trusting a lover who strays by and by

It's a child's game to ignore the pressures of strangers
only a fool's rememberer can prepare for the dangers

A voice sends messages from the mysterious second air
and I ward off the influences as if I didn't care

Yet while I look ahead I look over my shoulder
knowing too well the anticipation makes me grow older

As I pass by the storefront windows all in line
I see that my shadow's profile is not the same as mine

While auras of honesty fade in and out of view
I suspect I am surrounded by the chosen few

The promises they make leave me unfulfilled
and the secrets they share only challenge my will

I grow impatient waiting for an irrevocable offer
and as I wait, I grow increasingly stronger

I wonder, what would it take for a confrontation
could it be they exist only in my imagination

As the Moon pulls on tides, I feel the tug of persuasion
they are skilled opponents in this game of invasion

Memories of Nostradamos seek sanctity in my mind
as if I could solve the mysteries were I so inclined

It may be strange that I hold no regard for the skeptical
and for those who challenge my feelings as imperceptible

Because if their images were suddenly to disappear
I would have to ask myself, where they ever really here

BEFORE OUR FUTURE

Why are the whales dying on our beaches
Why is their survival beyond our reaches
Why have we not learned from those who teach us
Why can't we see what we've been told before

The hillsides are brown, the fields are dry
There's a filmy haze disguising the sky
We're fighting nature and we're wondering why
It's screaming from its very core

The sea lion has a look in his eye
He can't understand why his companions die
He knows we could help if we would only try
If only we had listened before

The ground shakes and the shorelines shiver
Every little creek becomes a river
The wildlife hide and begin to quiver
They've been through this before

Once free to roam and share the Earth
Our creatures are beginning to die at birth
What are we paying and what is it worth
We must know what is in store

Though the world will survive another season
Our indifference is nothing short of treason
Whatever happened to our sense of reason
Why didn't we listen before

Let's not learn from the past, some say
If destruction must come, it will be some other day
It's easier isn't it to look the other way
Who will remember what it was like before

PRESIDENTIAL WOE

For all the glory and wishes of luck
at the mercy of leaders who pass the buck
providing the bedding with the feathers you pluck
can you balance that weight on your shoulder?

Who'll stand behind you when reckoning comes
who will applaud you—who will you shun
How will you know whether you've lost or won
and still balance that weight on your shoulder

The gracious hosts now turn cold as stone
no one worth waving at will throw you a bone
your hand shakes as it rests on the telephone
and someone looks over your shoulder

Statements are made, promises broken
too late to take back the words you have spoken
We're certain to find the game marked by your token
as you seem to grow increasingly bolder

The maze has swallowed you—there's no way out
reality has faded leaving nothing but doubt
What is there left you can't do without
What is it you see over your shoulder

Make believe treaties are cause for concern
there are too many formulas for everyone to learn
and not enough candles are there left to burn
just a feeling of growing older

Guarding the secrets don't make you immune
you're equal to the target of a whaler's harpoon
The strings of harmony are no longer in tune
Have you felt it grow suddenly colder

Would you stop in the middle of this lonely road
would you exit the doors of your protected abode
Would you be grateful for someone to carry your load
and would you allow him to lean on your shoulder

But why give up now, so much left to do
imaginary boundaries should never stop you
Life will go on in spite of a few
as you keep looking over your shoulder

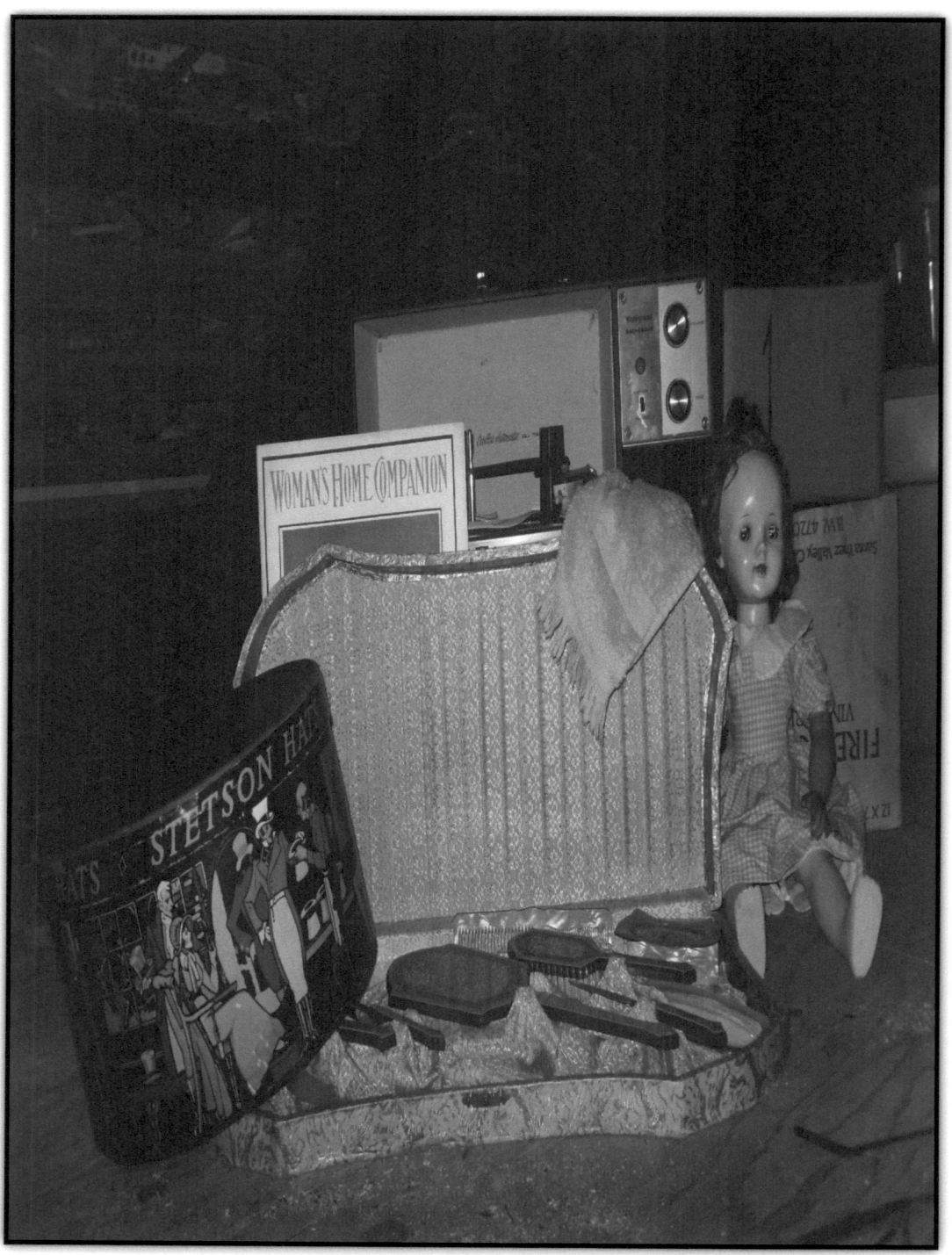

THE ATTIC

In the attic I found gifts of indeterminable proportions
full of worldly displays and unexplainable distortions

On dusty boards there lay secrets of the past
which obviously someone thought would last and last

In the hearts of others they represent boundless treasure
and pondering their existence gives me a strange sort of pleasure

I hear an echo of loneliness and another of pride
and there are boxes which seem to beckon me to look inside

I won't allow myself of think about what I might find
or their connection to the strangers who left all this behind

Yet a little closer look seems like such a small invasion
and might offer a clue to some timeless relation

Do all memories belong to their original creators
or am I on center stage in an empty theatre

Will I misinterpret someone else's possessions
Will I uncover truths, mysteries or confessions

My instinct tells me, and it wisely does
it's better I leave this attic exactly as it was

THE SANTA FE MUSIC HALL

presents

Open mic with featured reader.

Poetry

From Washington D.C. — QUIQUE AVILES

Allowed

Hosted by JOE RAY SANDOVAL

$3

STARRING MR SANDY

TUESDAY, APRIL 29, 9:00 P.M.

21 and over

SANTA FE MUSIC HALL 100 North Guadalupe 983-3311

CREATIVE CRITICISM

Expression explodes from challenges met
reflecting glory or echoing regret
Breaking away, shadowing a trend
leaving or attending souls on the mend

Artistry, in whatever form it takes
comes to a halt when someone applies the brakes
Overcome by the influence of power
talent tends to turn from sweet to sour

The spiritual gift of artistic creation
can become shattered by the realization
Another entity can control your thoughts
Art is a commodity now purchased in lots

Someone backs you
Millions are made
Promote yourself
Become second grade

Trade yourself
They'll pay you well
They'll promise anything
If they think you'll sell

So what is real and comes from the heart
is for whatever reason not accepted as art
The dealmakers know what's best for sure
art must be something more than pure

Masters of beauty, born of mystery
belong in the pages of history
What comes through them should be unconfined
their stores must be allowed to unwind

Without restriction in any respect
let the beholders decide what they expect
Who pays the way, who will be denied
what would you be without the talent you hide

Preferring profits over acclaimations
yet expecting both in your imaginations
You, who reap the rewards of the lease
have yet to create a masterpiece

Your conscience just might still awaken
one day your position could be shaken
Paint your own picture, write your own song
see if your talent will last that long

VIRGINITY

It's as though it were cast of the purest gold
and left alone on some fertile land
Without intrigue or deception, it stood all on its own
and was unquestionably in demand

Its desire to remain untouched is great
and its value historically more
but this fragile ego would have been lost at sea
had it not been washed ashore

It welcomes the feel of quality
fears theft by one who does not deserve
It wants no inhibitions, no definite conditions
as it lies waiting in reserve

In its search for perfection, it becomes impatient
and begins to weigh the risks
but it knows nothing of the danger and strife
that only inexperience inflicts

So it ventures out with heart in hand
disclaiming its inheritance
It soon becomes the target of wolves
who destroy its magnificence

Maybe you will find it sheltered somewhere
licking its wounds in retreat
but even now that it is tarnished, its head is held high
for its life is now complete

MESSAGE FOR DYLAN

Mystical, magical master of words
Someone left a message for you
It flies on the wings of a misguided bird
Determined to find a way through

It's an unwritten song, it's a make-believe dream
Camouflaged, wrinkled and blurred
But somehow I'm sure you will know what it means
Mystical, magical master of words

Carved into granite, baked into sand
Older than all in its time
There are no hidden promises in its steadying hand
Only gracious acceptance and rhyme

Mystical, magical master of words
It's a message meant only for you
You won't find it floating in the memories you stir
But maybe in some that are true

What will it tell you that you don't already know
Will it ease the pain you've endured
Will it open the doors to where you want to go
Mystical, magical master of words

Born as the best of our intellect
It will not be wasted on less
It has passed over idols for one with respect
Through a dreamer with much to confess

Mystical, magical master of words
It's a message that you could have sent
Some other time, some other world
When all other words had been spent

Just when you've pulled in your markers on call
You'll be wondering why you made that choice
Satisfaction comes from experiencing it all
Like the words that accompany your voice

You could leave the solitude undisturbed
And ignore what's meant only for you
But you may find your shadow on a red-painted curb
Selling its soul for a clue

Mystical, magical master of words
One day you'll discover it's true
You may not believe it, you may not have heard
That I left the message for you

OLD DAYS

Why am I reminded of the casual evenings
sitting by the fire with friends
and of the deeply philosophical conversations
that never seemed to come to an end

What was it that brought us together
what made us think we had something to share
There were so many other things we should have been doing
yet we passed the time without a care

We were soothed by a bottle of white wine and guitars
while sometimes angered by personal stress
It was so easy then just to ignore the days
and explore the nights without rest

It didn't matter if someone was waiting at home
we didn't need reasons to stay
It didn't seem logical to discuss tomorrow
when all that really mattered was today

Yet tomorrow did come
our times together began to fade
still there are thoughts and memories of the old days
which no stranger can ever invade

Now when I sit alone by the fire
I'm so grateful to be reminded of those friends
For it is then that I know those magical evenings
will never really come to an end

MY PLACE

Sometimes the only thing I can do is write words across the pages
as my thoughts wander aimlessly in stages and I daydream…
about what might have been

Then I catch myself drifting to some magical place
and know that I must not linger in this space as I daydream…
about what could be

Leave me alone in this place I have found
there's no reason for you to be looking around
I'll only be here for a while

Against my better judgment, I let my fantasies unroll
yet through it all I fight to keep control of my daydreams…
and where they might lead

I don't look for solutions for I know they're not here, but
there are no intrusions and things that I fear, only daydreams…
and I like what I see

Leave me alone in this place I have found
there's no reason for you to be hanging around
I'll only be here for a while

Suddenly the clock strikes as it passes the hour
and I know I must relinquish this imaginary power
as my daydreams…become reality

As for you, you will never knew I was gone
spending the whole time wondering what went wrong
because your daydreams…don't include me

And if you should find me in some dream come true
it will be because you had nothing else to do
when your daydreams…let you down

Leave me alone in this place I have found
please don't be following me around
I'll only be here for a while

What seemed like days was only minutes in fact
and I felt it was much too soon to be back
I was only there for a while

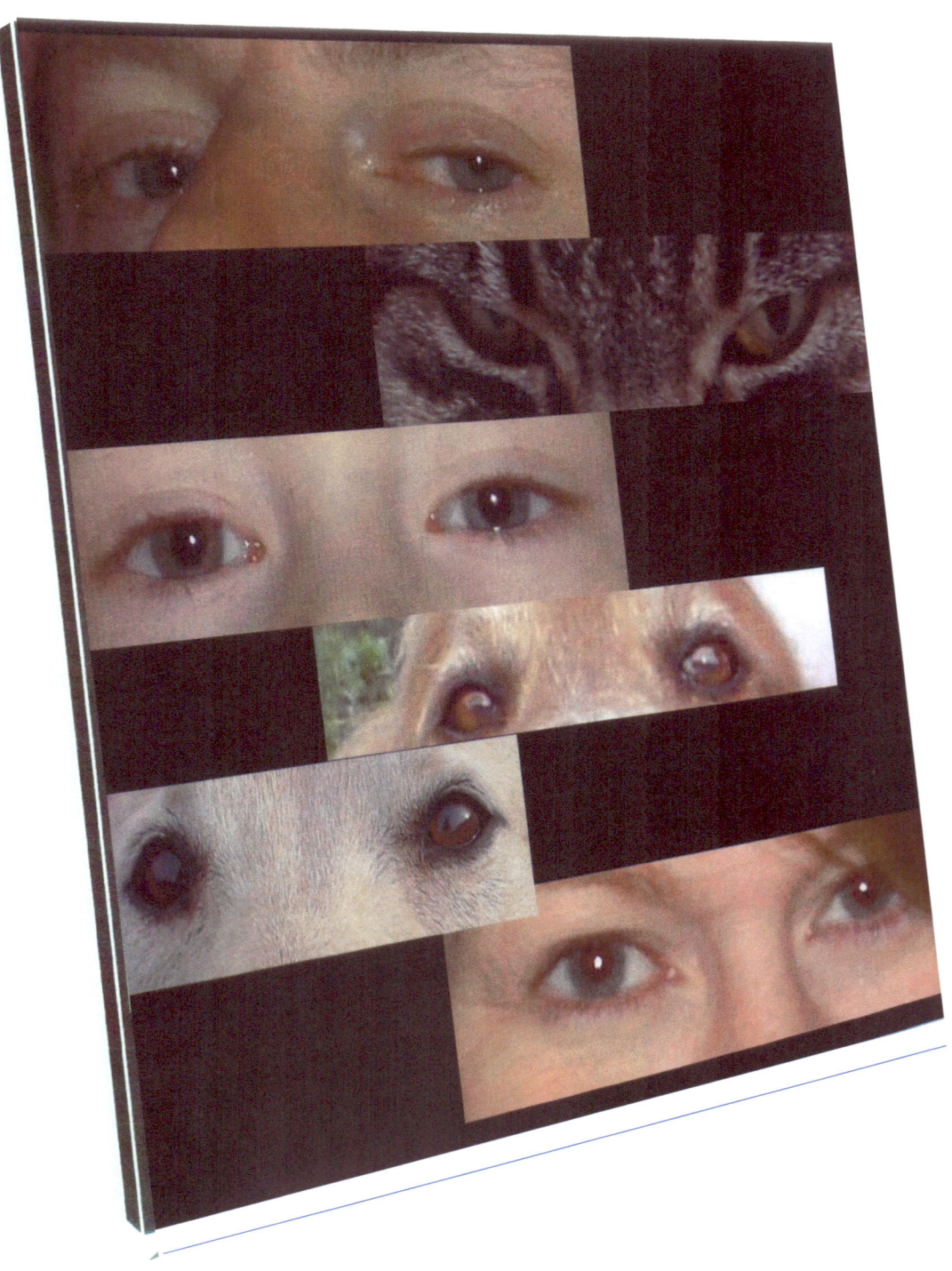

FULFILLMENT

As the years pass, we experience life
travel a road of both success and strife
Cherishing the union of husband and wife
wanting our hearts to be full

We care for our business, our beloved pets
we raise our children with few regrets
We keep our promises, we pay our debts
hoping our hearts will be full

We always hope we will learn from the wise
if we're let down, we reach for the skies
We separate ourselves from falsehood and lies
waiting for our hearts to be full

In the rarest of times we meet friends on the way
those who will listen to what we have to say
Who will understand and like us anyway
and finally, our hearts are full

GYPSY NOTES

It is with great pleasure that I acknowledge my dear friend, Susan Proctor, who has, as she puts it, "signed on" to collaborate with me to take this book wherever it may go. She took painstaking hours, not only to read my writings for the first time, but also assisting me in making it artistic and unusual, putting everything in perspective, and most of all giving me the encouraging (almost demanding) daily motivations to finish this wonderful endeavor we have embarked upon. It is also for special reasons that I acknowledge my son, Alan, his wife, Patty, and my grandson, Aedan, for their encouragement and the most important purpose that I wish to envelope in this everlasting legacy.

I also wish to thank my dear friend, Barbara Riley, as well as her husband, John, who with much determination, photographed the attic and the full moon. This is not to say I have forgotten about the abundance of friends who have, through the years, encouraged me to share my writings—Tony, Max and Irma, Pat and Diane, Stephanie, Marleen, Rowland, Christine, Joan, Rick, Mary, Sandy—to name a few. Each and every one of my friends have, in their own way, given me the courage to go forward—not only with this book—but also with my life. I thank each and every one of you—you know who you are—and this book is really dedicated to you.

www.ingramcontent.com/pod-product-compliance
Lightning Source LLC
Chambersburg PA
CBHW042030150426
43199CB00002B/17